Words *of* the Spirit

A collection of Poems

Featuring the new Covid Plandemic Poem, "Freedom Lost"

R.G. Hurst

Tampa, Florida

The views and opinions expressed in this book are solely those of the author and do not reflect the views or opinions of Gatekeeper Press. Gatekeeper Press is not to be held responsible for and expressly disclaims responsibility for the content herein.

Words of the Spirit

Published by Gatekeeper Press
7853 Gunn Hwy., Suite 209
Tampa, FL 33626
www.GatekeeperPress.com

Copyright © 2024 by R.G. Hurst
All rights reserved. Neither this book, nor any parts within it may be sold or reproduced in any form or by any electronic or mechanical means, including information storage and retrieval systems, without permission in writing from the author. The only exception is by a reviewer, who may quote short excerpts in a review.

Library of Congress Control Number: 2023942585

ISBN (paperback): 9781662939464

Dedications

Above all, I dedicate this little book to Jesus Christ, my rock and savior Without Him, there would be no poetry nor inspiration for it's creation.

I also dedicate it to Charotte Taylor, my now deceased mother, who has always supported me in everything I did and tried to do in life. I miss her greatly.

Preface

Proverbs 25:11 KJV

"A word fitly spoken is like apples of gold in pictures of Silver"

Poetry is the language of the soul. Only the truly inspired can use it, and the message it conveys goes much deeper than man's daily discourse. What better tool to explore the inner depths of the human mind? This work is a small collection of my most favorite poems with a little information on the authors. In addition, I have included a few of my own newly released poems. I hope you find them inspiring.

Contents

An Old Story by Edwin Robinson	1
For Whom the Bell Tolls by John Donne	3
Ghost of the Murdered by R.G. Hurst	5
Invictus by William Ernest Henley	7
The Tiger by William Blake	9
The Lamb by William Blake	11
Freedom Lost by R.G. Hurst	12
Richard Cory by Edwin Arlington Robinson	13
The Raven by Edgar Allan Poe	14
The Last Word by Matthew Arnold	20
In Nocte by R.G. Hurst	22
Crossing the Bar by Alfred Lord Tennyson	23
Ode to Intimations of Immortality by William Wordsworth	25
Rime of the Ancient Mariner - by Samuel Taylor Coleridge	35
Grey Lady by R.G. Hurst	42
After Word - Epilogue	43

An Old Story

Strange that I did not know him then,
   That friend of mine!
I did not even show him then
   One friendly sign;

But cursed him for the ways he had
   To make me see
My envy of the praise he had
   For praising me.

I would have rid the earth of him
   Once, in my pride!....
I never knew the worth of him
   Until he died.

                                        Edwin Arlington Robinson

Edwin Arlington Robinson

Edwin Arlington Robinson (December 22, 1869 — April 6, 1935) was an American poet. He was born in Lincoln County, Maine, but his family moved to Gardiner, Maine, in 1871. He described his childhood in Maine as "stark and unhappy". His parents had wanted a girl, and did not name him until he was six months old, when they visited a holiday resort - at which point other vacationers decided that he should have a name, and selected the name "Edwin" from a hat containing a random set of boy's names. The man who drew the name was from Arlington, Massachusetts, so "Arlington" was used for his middle name. Throughout his life, he hated not only his given name but also his family's habit of calling him "Win". As an adult, he always used the signature "E.A." He once wrote in a letter to a friend " writing has been my dream ever since I was old enough to lay a plan for an air castle" Robinson's early struggles led many of his poems to have a dark pessimism and his stories to be likewise influenced. His eldest brother, Dean, was a doctor and had become addicted to laudanum while self-medicating for neuralgia. His middle brother, Herman, a handsome and charismatic man, married the woman Edwin loved, Emma Loehen Shepherd, leaving him despondent. Emma thought highly of Edwin, and encouraged his portry but he was deemed too young to be in competition for her hand. This did not keep him from being agitated deeply by witnessing what he considered her being deceived by Herman's charm and choosing shallowness over depth. Robinson won the Pulitzer Prize for Poetry on three occasions and was nominated for the Nobel Prize in Literature four times.. He never married and died of cancer on April 6, 1935, in a New York hospital.

For Whom the Bell Tolls

No man is an island,
Entire of itself.
Each is a piece of the continent,
A part of the main.
If a clod be washed away by the sea,
Europe is the less.
As well as if a promontory were,
As well as if a manor of thine own
Or of thine friend's were.
Each man's death diminishes me,
For I am involved in mankind.
Therefore, send not to know
For whom the bell tolls,
It tolls for thee.

John Donne

John Donne

John Donne was born in 1572 in London, England. He is known as the founder of the Metaphysical Poets, a term created by Samuel Johnson, an eighteenth-century English essayist, poet, and philosopher. The loosely associated group also includes George Herbert, Richard Crashaw, Andrew Marvell, and John Cleveland. The Metaphysical Poets are known for their ability to startle the reader and coax new perspective through paradoxical images, suble argument, inventive syntax, and imagery from art, philosophy, and religion using an extended metaphor known as a conceit. Donne often employs conceits, or extended metaphors, to yoke together "heterogenous ideas," in the words of Samuel Johnson, thus generating the powerful ambiguity for which his work is famous. This reached beyond the rational and hierarchical structure of the seventeenth century. His work is distinguished by its emotional and sonic intensity and its capacity to plumb the paradoxes of faith, human and divine love, and the possibility of salvation. In Donne's own day his poetry was highly prized among the small circle of his admirers, who read it as it was circulated in manuscript. In his later years he gained wide fame as a preacher..Donne entered the world during a period of theological and political unrest for both England and France; a Protestant massacre occurred on Saint Bartholomew's day in France; while in England, the Catholics were the persecuted minority. Born into a Roman Catholic family, Donne's personal relationship with religion was tumultuous and passionate, and at the center of much of his poetry. He studied at both Oxford and Cambridge Universities in his early teen years but did not take a degree at either school, because to do so would have meant subscribing to the Thirty-nine Articles, the doctrine that defined Anglicanism. At age twenty, he studied law at Lincoln's Inn. Two years later he succumbed to religious pressure and joined the Anglican Church after his younger brother, convicted for his catholic loyalties, died in prison. In 1601 Donne secretly married Anne More, with whom he had twelve children. In 1615 he was ordained Anglican deacon and then priest, although he did not want to take holy orders and only did so because the King ordered it.

Ghost of the Murdered

Sum quod eris

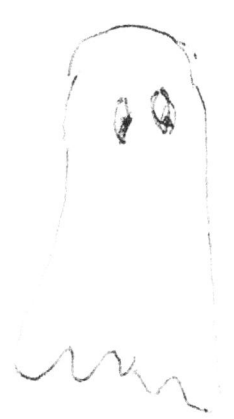

Walked I once the earth in all it's glory,
Did hear and feel and see
Now linger I in the cold, damp ground.
I am what you shall be.

Tears and fears in psychic repose
Can misdirect the will of man
When struggling with the forces from below.
Is best to know where you stand.

Alas, too late; unshielded came you a fort night since
And did strip my soul from my body free.
Now I thread the chambers of the dead
Waiting to greet thee.

R.G. Hurst

R.G. Hurst

R.G. Hurst is a 21st century American poet raised in the rural upper South along the Clinch River and loves to explore the outdoors and commune with nature. A graduate of Prince George High, Hurst later attended ODU and MCV as well as Shenandoah University. Trained and employed in the medical field, Hurst is now retired and conducting independent research in natural healing/treatment modalities.

Invictus

Out of the night that covers me,
Black as the pit from pole to pole,
I thank whatever gods may be
For my unconquerable soul.

In the fell clutch of circumstance
I have not winced nor cried aloud.
Under the bludgeonings of chance
My head is bloody, but unbowed.

Beyond this place of wrath and tears
Looms but the Horror of the shade,
And yet the menace of the years
Finds, and shall find, me unafraid.

It matters not how strait the gate,
How charged with punishments the scroll,
I am the master of my fate:
I am the captain of my soul.

William Ernest Henley

William Ernest Henley

William Ernest Henley (1849-1903) was an English poet, editor, and critic. His father was a struggling bookseller who died when Henley was a teenager. At the age of 12 Henley was diagnosed with tubercular arthritis that necessitated the amputation of one of his legs just below the knee; the other foot was saved only through a radical surgery performed by Joseph Lister. As he healed in the infirmary, Henley began to write poems, including "Invictus". Henley's poems often engage themes of inner strength and perseverance. He was a close friend of Robert Louis Stevenson, who reportedly based his Long John Silver character in "Treasure Island" in part on Henley.

The Tiger

Tiger Tiger, burning bright,
In the forests of the night;
What immortal hand or eye,
Could frame thy fearful symmetry?

In what distant deeps or skies,
Burnt the fire of thine eyes?
On what wings dare he aspire?
What the hand, dare seize the fire?

And what shoulder, & what art,
Could twist the sinews of thy heart?
And when thy heart began to beat,
What dread hand? & what dread feet?

What the hammer? what the chain,
In what furnace was thy brain?
What the anvil? what dread grasp,
Pare its deadly terrors clasp!

When the stars threw down their spears
And water'd heaven with their tears:
Did he smile his work to see?
Did he who made the Lamb make thee?

Tiger Tiger, burning bright,
In the forests of the night:
What immortal hand or eye,
Dare frame thy fearful symmetry?

by William Blake

William Blake

William Blake (28 November 1757 - 12 August 1827) was an English poet, painter, and printmaker. He was a committed Christian who was hostile to the Church of England and almost all froms of organized religion. From early childhood, Blake spoke of having visions — at four he saw God "put his head to the window"; around age nine, while walking through the countryside, he saw a tree filled with angels. Although his parents tried to discourage him from "lying", they did observe that he was different from his peers and did not force him to attend a conventional school. Instead he learned to read and write at home. At age ten, Blake expressed a wish to become a painter; so his parents sent him to drawing school. Two years later, Blake begin writing poetry. Blake" was largely unrecognized during his life, and even considered mad by contemporaries for his idiosyncratic views. Later critics , however, held him in high regard for his expressiveness and creativity, and for the philosophical and mystical undercurrents within his work. His paitings and poetry have been characterised as part of the Romantic movement and as "Pre-Romantic".

The Lamb

Little Lamb who made thee
    Dost thou know who made thee
Gave thee life & bid thee feed,
By the stream & o'er the mead;
Gave thee clothing of delight,
Softest clothing wooly bright;
Gave thee such a tender voice,
Making all the vales rejoice!
    Little Lamb who made thee
    Dost thou know who made thee

    Little Lamb I'll tell thee,
    Little Lamb I'll tell thee!
He is called by thy name,
For he calls himself a Lamb:
He is meek and he is mild,
He became a little child:
I a child & thou a lamb,
We are called by his name.
    Little Lamb God bless thee.
    Little Lamb God bless thee.

by William Blake

Freedom Lost

(The Covid Plandemic Poem)

When reason leaves through door of fear
Choice once was, is not your own
Surrendered to the Lower Power
Darkness seeking to rob your throne

Faceless faces seen where ever you go
Masked from without, sorcery injected within
Sheep obedient to a voice they don't know
Decisions forged in fear, most always a sin.

Join not the chaos, struggle and strife
Believe not the lies those in power shall tier
Were you not long warned by the Book of life
Stay safe in His grace, let the lost follow fear.

If He be in you, stand fast and strong
Protect the Temple and all within
Let them when the Savior comes,
Reap the horrors they did begin.

R.G. Hurst

Richard Cory

Whenever Richard Cory went down town,
We people on the pavement looked at him:
He was a gentleman from sole to crown,
Clean favored, and imperially slim.

And he was always quietly arrayed,
And he was always human when he talked;
Buut still he fluttered pulses when he said,
"Good-morning," and he glittered when he walked.

And he was rich - yes, richer than a king -
And admirably schooled in every grace:
In fine, we thought that he was everything
To make us wish that we were in his place.

So on we worked, and waited for the Hight,
And went without the meat, and cursed the bread;
And Richard Cory, one calm summer night,
Went home and put a bullet through his head.

By Edwin Arlington Robinson

The Raven

Once upon a midnight dreary, while I pondered, weak, and weary,
Over many a quaint and curious volume of forgotten lore—
While I nodded, nearly napping, suddenly there came a tapping,
As of some one gently rapping, rapping, at my chamber door.
"Tis some visitor," I muttered, "tapping at my chamber door—
      Only this and nothing more."

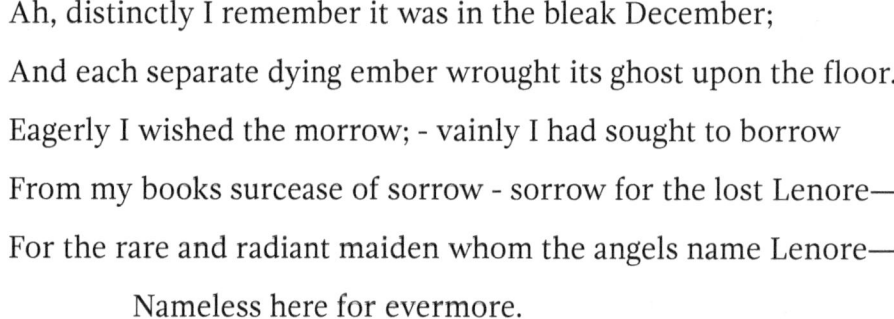

Ah, distinctly I remember it was in the bleak December;
And each separate dying ember wrought its ghost upon the floor.
Eagerly I wished the morrow; - vainly I had sought to borrow
From my books surcease of sorrow - sorrow for the lost Lenore—
For the rare and radiant maiden whom the angels name Lenore—
      Nameless here for evermore.

And the silken, sad, uncertain rustling of each purple curtain
Thrilled me - filled me with fantastic terrors never felt before;
So that now, to still the beating of my heart, I stood repeating
"Tis some visitor entreating entrance at my chamber door -
Some late visitor entreating entrance at my chamber door;--
      This it is and nothing more."

Presently my soul grew stronger; hesitating then no longer,

"Sir," said I, "or Madam, truly your forgiveness I implore;

But the fact is I was napping, and so gently you came rapping,

And so faintly you came tapping, tapping at my chamber door,

That I scare was sure I heard you" - here I opened wide the door;--

      Darkness there and nothing more.

Deep into that darkness peering, long I stood there wondering, fearing,

Doubting, dreaming dreams no mortal ever dared to dream before;

But the silence was unbroken, and the stillness gave no token,

And the only word there spoken was the whispered word, "Lenore?"

This I whispered, and an echo murmured back the word, "Lenore!" –

      Merely this and nothing more.

Back into the chamber turning, all my soul within me burning,

Soon again I hear a tapping somewhat louder than before.

"Surely," said I, "surely that is something at my window lattice;

Let me see, then, what thereat is, and this mystery explore -

      "Tis the wind and nothing more!"

Open here I flung the shutter, when, with many a flirt and flutter,

In there stepped a stately Raven of the saintly days of yore;

Not the least obeisance made he; not a minute stopped or stayed he;

But, with mien of lord or lady, perched above my chamber door-

Perched upon a bust of Pallas just above my chamber door -

      Perched, and sat, and nothing more.

Then this ebony bird beguiling my sad fancy into smiling,

By the grave and stern decorum of the countenance it wore,

"Though thy crest be shorn and shaven, thou, " I said, " art sure no craven,

Ghastly grim and ancient Raven wandering, from the Nightly shore—

Tell me what thy lordly name is on the Night's Plutonian shore!"

        Quoth the Raven "Nevermore."

Much I marvelled this ungainly fowl to hear discourse so plainly,

Though its answer little meaning - little relevancy bore;

For we cannot help agreeing that no living human being

Ever yet was blessed with seeing bird above his chamber door—

Bird or beast upon the culptured bust above his chamber door,

        With such name as "Nevermore."

But the Raven, sitting lonely on the placid bust, spoke only

That one word, as if his soul in that one word he did outpour.

Nothing farther then he uttered—not a feather then he fluttered—

Till I scarcely more than muttered "Other friends have flown before—

On the morrow he will leave me, as my Hopes have flown before."

        Then the bird said "Nevermore."

Startled at the stillness broken by reply so aptly spoken,

"Doubtless," said l,, "what it utters is its only stock and store

Caught from some unhappy master whom unmerciful Disaster

Followed fast and followed faster till his songs one burden bore—

Till the dirges of his Hope that melancholy burden bore

        Of 'Never—nevermore'."

But the Raven still beguiling, all my fancy into smiling,

Straight I wheeled a cushioned seat in front of bird, and bust and door;

Then, upon the velvet sinking, I betook myself to linking

Fancy unto fancy, thinking what this ominous bird of yore—

What this grim, ungainly, ghastly, gaunt, and ominous bird of yore

   Meant in croaking, "Nevermore."

This I sat engaged in guessing, but no syllable expressing

To the fowl whose fiery eyes now burned into my bosom's core;

This and more I sat divining, with my head at ease reclining

On the cushion's velvet lining that the lamp-light gloated o'er

But whose velvet-violet lining with the lamp-light gloating, o'er,

   She shall press, ah, nevermore!

Then, methought, the air grew denser, perfumed from an unseen censer

Swung by Seraphim whose foot-falls tinkled on the tufted floor.

"Wretch," I cried, "thy God hath lent thee - by these angels he hath sent thee

Respite - respite and nepenthe from thy memories of Lenore;

Quaff, oh quaff this kind nepenthe and forget this lost Lenore!"

   Quoth the Raven "Nevermore."

"Prophet!" said I, "thing of evil! - prophet still, if bird or devil!—

Whether Tempter sent, or whether tempest tossed thee here ashore,

Desolate yet all undaunted, on this desert land enchanted—

On this home by Horror haunted - tell me truly, I implore—

Is there - is there balm in Gilead? - tell me - tell me, I implore!"

   Quoth the Raven "Nevermore."

"Prophet!" said I, "thing of evil! - prophet still, if bird or devil!

By that Heaven that bends above us - by that God we both adore—

Tell this soul with sorrow laden if, within the distant, Aidenn,

It shall clasp a sainted maiden whom the angels name Lenore—

Clasp a rare and radiant maiden whom the angels name Lenore."

    Quoth the Raven "Nevermore."

"Be that word our sign of parting, bird or fiend!" I shrieked, upstarting—

"Get thee back into the tempest and the Night's Plutonian shore!

Leave no black plume as a token of that lie thy soul hath spoken!

Leave my loneliness unbroken! - quit the bust above my door!

Take thy beak from out my heart, and take thy form from off my door!"

    Quoth the Raven "Nevermore."

And the Raven, never flitting, still is sitting, still is sitting,

On the pallid bust of Pallas just above my chamber door;

And his eyes have all the seeming, of a demon's that is dreaming,

And the lamp-light o'er him streaming throws his shadow on the floor;

And my soul from out that shadow that lies floating on the floor

    Shall be lifted - nevermore!

By Edgar Allan Poe

Edgar Allan Poe

Edgar Allan Poe (January 19, 1809 - October 7, 1849) was an American 'writer, poet, editor, and literary critic best known for his poetry and short stories, particularly his tales of mystery and the macabre. He is widely regarded as a central figure of Romanticism in the United States, and of American literature.. he was born in Boston. His father abandoned the family in 1810, and when his mother died the following year, Poe was taken in by John and Frances Allan of Richmond Virginia. They never formerly adopted him, but he was with them well into young adulthood. In 1836 he married his 13-year-old cousin, Virginia Clemm, but she died of tuberculosis in 1847. After Virginia's death Poe's lifelong struggle with depression and alcoholism worsened. Poe's death was mysterious. On October 3, 1849 he was found semiconscious in Baltimore, " in great distress, and ...in need of immediate assistance", acccording to Joseph W. Walker, who found him. He was taken to the Washington Medical College, where he died on Sunday, October 7, 1849 at 5 in the morning. Poe was not coherent long enough to explain how he come to be in his dire condition and why he was wearing clothes that were not his own. He is said to have repeataedly called out the name " Reynolds" on the night before his death, though it is unclear to whom he was referring. Newspapers at the time reported Poe's death as 'congestion of the brain' or "cerebral inflammation", common euphemisms for death from disreputable causes such as alcoholism. The actual cause of death remains a mystery. Speculation has included delirium tremens, heart disease, epilepsy, syphilis, meningeal inflammation, cholera, carbon monoxide poisoning, and rabies. One theory dating from 1872 suggests that Poe's death resulted from cooping, a form of electoral fraud in which citizens were forced to vote for a particular candidate, sometimes leading to violence and even murder. All of the relevant medical records have been lost, including Poe's death certificate.

The Last Word

Creep into thy narrow bed

Creep and let no more be said

Vain thy onset all stands fast

Thou thyself must break at last

Let the long contentions cease

Geese are swans and swans are geese

Let them have it as they will

Thou art tired, best be still

They out talked thee, hissed thee, tore thee

Better men faired thus before thee

Fired their ringing shot and passed

Hotly charged and sank at last

Charge once more then and be dumb

Let the victors when they come

When thy forts of folly fall

Find thy body by the wall

By Matthew Arnold

Matthew Arnold

Matthew Arnold (24 December 1822 – 15 April 1888) was an English poet and cultural critic who worked as an inspector of schools. He was the son of Thomas Arnold, the celebrated headmaster of Rugby School, and brother to both Tom Arnold, literary professor, and William Delafield Arnold, novelist and colonial administrator. He was also an inspector of schools for thirty-five years, and supported the concept of state-regulated secondary education. Arnold, however, often described his duties as a school inspector a 'drudgery" although " at other times he acknowledged the benefit of regular work". Arnold was elected Professor of Poetry at Oxford in 1857, and he was the first in this position to deliver his lectures in English rather than in Latin. He was re-elected in 1862. Matthew Arnold has been characterized as a sage writer, a type of writer who chastises and instructs the reader on contemporary social issues. Arnold is sometimes called the third great Victorian poet, along with Alfred Lord Tennyson, and Robert Browning. Arnold died suddenly in 1888 of heart failure whilst running to meet a train that would have taken him to the Liverpool Landing Stage to see his daughter, who was visiting from the United States where she had moved after marrying an American. He was survived by his wife, who died in June 1901.

In Nocte

Rowing across the shores of life
In the darkness as we came
We hardly know as once before
And die in darkness, as the same.

All knowledge left far behind
Man tries to gain it back, somehow
He riths in doubt, he shrieks in pain,
With misery is his life endowed.

Glancing to see the star lit sky
In the cool cloak of night we sit.
Herein we cry, the truth must lie.
We try remember, yet forget.

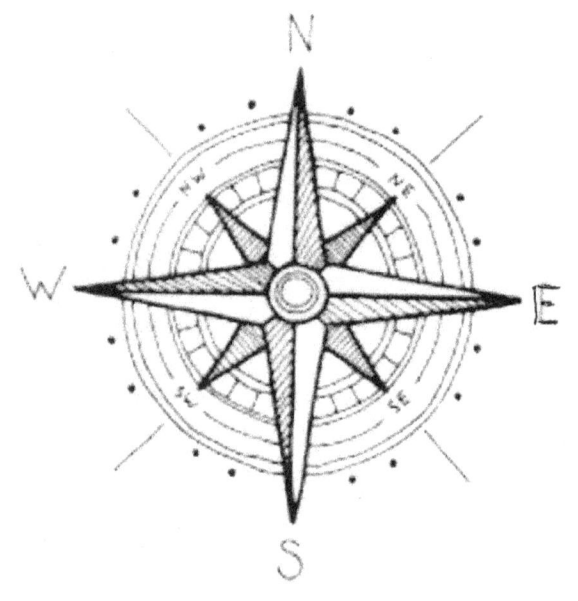

With fleshy birth of life is launched
A crooked rudder for the soul,
And swerves far from straight, the prison ship
As o'er the tossing waves it tows.

Then frightful storms oft rise at sea
In ignorance, fear we of the deep.
As such we cannot 'banden ship,
In weary sickness, on we sleep.

At length, at last, the port is reached
Then with the key of death is wide
The prison doors which bound souls tight
To purest knowledge then we glide.

R.G. Hurst

Crossing the Bar

Sunset and evening star,
    And one clear call for me!
And may there be no moaning of the bar,
    When I put out to sea.

But such a tide as moving seems asleep,
    Too full for sound and foam,
When that which drew from out the boundless deep
    Turns again home.

Twilight and evening bell,
    And after that the dark!
And may there be no sadness of farewell,
    When I embark;

For tho' from out our bourne of Time and Place
    The flood may bear me far,
I hope to see my Pilot face to face
    When I have crost the bar.

By Alfred Lord Tennyson

Alfred Lord Tennyson

Alfred Lord Tennyson (1809 – 1892) is one of the most well - loved Victorian poets. He was born in Somersby, Lincolnshire, England the fourth of twelve children. Some knowledge of the lurid history of Tennyson's family is essential for understanding the recurrence in his poetry of themes of madness, murder, avarice, miserliness, social climbing, marriages arranged for profit instead of love, and estrangements between families and friends. Part of the family heritage was a strain of epilepsy, a disease then thought to be brought on by sexual excess and therefore shameful. One of Tennyson's brothers was confined to an insane asylum most of his life, another had recurrent bouts of addiction to drugs, a third had to be put into a mental home because of his alcoholism, another was intermittently confirned and died relatively young. Of the rest of the 11 children who reached maturity, ail had at least one severe mental breakdown. During the first half of his life, Alfred thought that he had inherited epilepsy from his father and that it was responsible for the trances into which he occasionally fell until he was well over 40 years old. It was in part to escape from the unhappy environment of Somersby rectory that Alfred begin writing poetry iong before he was sent to school, as did most of his talented brothers and sisters. All his life he used writing as a way of taking his mind from his troubles. One aspect of his method of composition was set, too, while he was still a boy: he would make up phrases or discrete lines as he walked and store them in his memory until he had a proper setting for them. He showed an early talent for writing. At age twelve he wrote a 6,000 line epic poem. Tennyson became one of Britain's most popular poets and was selected as poet laureate in succession to William Wordsworth.

Ode: Intimations of Immortality from Recollections of Early Childhood

The child is father of the man;

And I could wish my days to be

Bound each to each by natural piety

There was a time when meadow, grove, and stream,

The earth, and every common sight,

To me did seem

Apparelled in celestial light,

The glory and the freshness of a dream.

It is not now as it hath been of yore; -

Turn wheresoe'er I may,

By night or day.

The things which I have seen I now can see no more.

The Rainbow comes and goes,

And lovely is the Rose,

The Moon doth with delight

Look round her when the heavens are bare,

Waters on a starry night

Are beautiful and fair;

The sunshine is a glorious birth;

But yet I know, where'er I go,

That there hath past away a glory from the earth.

Now, while the birds thus sing a joyous song,

And while the young lambs bound

As to the tabor's sound,

To me along there came a thought of grief:

A timely utterance gave that thought relief,

And I again am strong:

The cataracts blow their trumpets from the steep;

No more shall grief of mine the season wrong;

I hear the Echoes through the mountains throng,

The Winds come to me from the fields of sleep,

And all the earth is gay;

Land and sea

Give themselves up to jollity,

And with the heart of May

Doth every Beast keep holiday; -

Thou Child of Joy,

Shout round me, let me hear thy shouts, thou happy Shepherd-boy.

Ye blessed creatures, I have heard the call

Ye to each other make; I see

The heavens laugh with you in your jubilee;

My heart is at your festival,

My head hath its coronal,

The fullness of your bliss, I feel - I feel it all.

Oh evil day! If I were sullen

While Earth herself is adorning,

This sweet May-morning,

And the Children are culling

On every side,

In a thousand valleys far and wide,

Fresh flowers; while the sun shines warm,

And the Babe leaps up on his Mother's arm: -

I hear, I hear, with joy I hear!

But there's a Tree, of many, one,

A single field which I have looked upon,

Both of them speak of something that is gone;

The Pansy at my feet

Doth the same tale repeat:

Whither is fled the visionary gleam?

Where is it now, the glory and the dream?

Our birth is but a sleep and a forgetting:

The Soul that rises with us, our life's Star,

Hath had elsewhere its setting,

And cometh from afar:

Not in entire forgetfulness,

And not in utter nakedness,

But trailing clouds of glory do we come

From God, who is our home:

Heaven lies about us in our infancy!

Shades of the prison-house begin to close

Upon the growing Boy,

But he beholds the light, and whence it flows,

He sees it in his joy;

The Youth, who daily farther from the east

Must travel, still is Nature's Priest,

And by the vision splendid

Is on his way attended;

At length the Man perceives it die away,

And fade into the light of common day.

Earth fills her lap with pleasures of her own;

Yearnings she hath in her own natural kind,

And, even with something of a Mother's mind,

And no unworthy aim,

The homely Nurse doth all she can

To make her Foster-child, her Inmate Man,

Forget the glories he hath known,

And that imperial palace whence he came.

Behold the Child among his new-born blisses,

A six years' Darling of a pygmy size!

See, where 'mid work of his own hand he lies,

Fretted by sallies of his mother's kisses,

With light upon him from his father's eyes!

See, at his feet, some little plan or chart,

Some fragment from his dream of human life,

Shaped by himself with newly-learned art

A wedding or a festival,

A mourning or a funeral;

And this hath now his heart,

And unto this he frames his song:

Then will he fit his tongue
To dialogues of business, love, or strife;
But it will not be long
Ere this be thrown aside,
And with new joy and pride
The little Actor cons another part;
Filling from time to time his "humorous stage"
With all the Persons, down to palsied Age,
That Life brings with her in her equipage;
As if his whole vocation
Were endless imitation.

Thou, whose exterior semblance doth belie
Thy Soul's immensity;
Thou best Philosopher, who yet dost keep
Thy heritage, thou Eye among the blind,
That, deaf and silent, read'st the eternal deep,
Haunted forever by the eternal mind, -
Mighty Prophet! Seer blest!
On whom those truths do rest,
Which we are toiling all our lives to find,
In darkness lost, the darkness of the grave;
Thou, over whom thy Immortality
Broods like the Day, a Master o'er a Slave,
A Presence which is not to be put by;
Thou little Child, yet glorious in the might

Of heaven-born freedom on thy being's height,
Why with such earnest pains dost thou provoke
The years to bring the inevitable yoke,
Thus blindly with thy blessedness at strife?
Full soon thy Soul shall have her earthly freight,
And custom lie upon thee with a weight,
Heavy as frost, and deep almost as life!

O joy! That in our embers
Is something that doth live,
That Nature yet remembers
What was so fugitive!
The thought of our past years in me doth breed
Perpetual benediction: not indeed
For that which is most worthy to be blest;
Delight and liberty, the simple creed
Of Childhood, whether busy or at rest,
With new-fledged hope still fluttering in his breast: --
Not for these I raise
The song of thanks and praise
But for those obstinate questionings
Of sense and outward things,
Fallings from us, vanishings;
Blank misgivings of a Creature
Moving about in worlds not realized,
High instincts before which our mortal Nature

Did tremble like a guilty thing surprised:
But for those first affections,
Those shadowy recollections,
Which, be they what they may
Are yet the fountain-light of all our day,
Are yet a master-light of all our seeing;
Uphold us, cherish, and have power to make
Our noisy years seem moments in the being
Of the eternal Silence: truths that wake,
To perish never;
Which neither listlessness, nor mad endeavor,
Nor Man nor Boy,
Nor all that is at enmity with joy,
Can utterly abolish or destroy!
Hence in a season of calm weather
Though inland far we be,
Our Souls have sight of that immortal sea
Which brought us hither,
Can in a moment travel thither,
And see the Children sport upon the shore,
And hear the mighty waters rolling evermore.

Then sing, ye Birds, sing, sing a joyous song!
And let the young Lambs bound
As to the tabor's sound!
We in thought will join your throng,

Ye that pipe and ye that play,

Ye that through your hearts to-day

Feel the gladness of the May!

What though the radiance which was once so bright

Be now forever taken from my sight,

Though nothing can bring back the hour

Of splendor in the grass, of glory in the flower;

We will grieve not, rather find

Strength in what remains behind;

In the primal sympathy

Which having been must ever be;

In the soothing thoughts that spring

Out of human suffering;

In the faith that looks through death,

In years that bring the philosophic mind.

And O, ye Fountains, Meadows, Hills, and Groves,

Forebode not any severing of our loves!

Yet in my heart of hearts I feel your might;

I only have relinquished one delight

To live beneath your more habitual sway.

I love the Brooks which down their channels fret,

Even more than when I tripped lightly as they;

The innocent brightness of a new-born Day

Is lovely yet;

The Clouds that gather round the setting sun

Do take a sober colouring from an eye

That hath kept watch o'er man's morality;

Another race hath been, and other palms are won.

Thanks to the human heart by which we live,

Thanks to its tenderness, its joys, and fears,

To me the meanest flower that blows can give

Thoughts that do often lie too deep for tears.

                                        By William Wordsworth

William Wordsworth

William Wordsworth (7 April 1770 – 23 April 1850), was an English Romantic poet who, with Samuel Taylor Coleridge, helped to launch the Romantic Age in English literature. He was born in Cockermouth Cumberland, located in the Lake District of England: an area that would become closely associated with Wordsworth for over 2 centuries after his death. He began writing poetry as a young boy in grammar school, and before graduating from college he went on a walking tour of Europe, which deepened his love for nature and his sympathy for the common man: both major themes in his poetry. He is remembered as a poet of spiritual and epistemological speculation, a poet oncerned with the human relationship to nature and a fierce advocate of using the vocabulary and speech patterns of common people in poetry. Wordsworth is best known for "Lyrical Ballads" co-written with Samuel Taylor Coleridge, and "The Prelude", a Romantic epic poem chronicling the "growth of a poet's mind." Wordsworth was Poet Laureate from 1843 until his death from pleurisy on 23 April 1850.

Rime of the Ancient Mariner (PART VII)

This Hermit good lives in that wood
Which slopes down to the sea.
How loudly his sweet voice he rears!
He loves to talk with marineres
That come from a far countree.

He kneels at morn, and noon, and eve-
He hath a cushion plump:
It is the moss that wholly hides
The rotted old oak-stump.

The skiff-boat neared: I heard them talk,
'Why, this is strange, I trow!
Where are those lights so many and fair,
That signal made but now?'

'Strange, by my faith!' the Hermit said-
'And they answered not our cheer!
The planks looked warped! And see those sails,
How thin they are and sere!
I never saw aught like to them,
Unless perchance it were

Brown skeletons of leaves that lag

My forest-brook along;

When the ivy-tod is heavy with snow,

And the owler whoops to the wolf below,

That eats the she-wolf's young.'

'Dear Lord! It hath a fiendish look -

(The Pilot made reply)

I am a-feared' -'Push on, push on!'

Said the Hermit cheerily.

The boat came closer to the ship,

But I nor spake nor stirred;

The boat came close beneath the ship,

And straight a sound was heard.

Under the water it rumbled on,

Still louder and more dread:

It reached the ship, it split the bay;

The ship went down like lead.

Stunned by that loud and dreadful sound,

Which sky and ocean smote,

Like one that hath been seven days drowned

My body lay afloat;

But swift as dreams, myself

I found Within the Pilot's boat.

Upon the whirl, where sank the ship,
The boat spun round and round;
And all was still, save that the hill
Was telling of the sound.

I moved my lips - the Pilot shrieked
And fell down in a fit;
The holy Hermit raised his eyes,
And prayed where he did sit.

I took the oars: the Pilot's boy,
Who now doth crazy go,
Laughed loud and long, and all the while
His eyes went to and fro.
'Ha! Ha!' quoth he, ' full plain I see,
The Devil knows how to row.'

And now, all in my own countree,
I stood on the firm land!
The Hermit stepped forth from the boat,
And scarcely he could stand.

'O shrieve me, shrieve me, holy man!'
The Hermit crossed his brow.
'Say quick,' quoth he, 'I bid thee say -
What manner of man art thou?'

Forthwith this frame of mine was wrenched
With a woeful agony
Which forced me to begin my tale:
And then it left me free.

Since then, at an uncertain hour,
That agony returns:
And till my ghastly tale is told,
This heart within me burns.

I pass, like night, from land to land:
I have strange power of speech;
That moment that his face I see,
I know the man that must hear me:
To him my tale I teach.

What loud uproar bursts from that door!
The wedding-guests are there:
But in the garden-bower the bride
And bride-maids singing are:
And hark the little vesper bell,
Which biddeth me to prayer!

O Wedding-Guest! This soul hath been
Alone on a wide wide sea:
So lonely 'twas, that God himself
Scarce seemed there to be.

O sweeter than the marriage-feast,
'Tis sweeter far to me,
To walk together to the kirk
With a goodly company! -

To walk together to the kirk,
And all together pray,
While each to his great Father bends,
Old men, and babes, and loving friends
And youths and maidens gay!

Farewell, farewell! But this I tell
To thee, thou Wedding-Guest!
He prayeth well, who loveth well
Both man and bird and beast.

He prayeth best, who loveth best
All things both great and small;
For the dear God who loveth us,
He made and loveth all.

The Mariner, whose eye is bright,
Whose beard with age is hoar,
Is gone: and now the Wedding-Guest
Turned from the bridegroom's door.

He went like one that hath been stunned,

And is of sense forlorn:

A sadder and a wiser man,

He rose the morrow morn.

                                        by Samuel Taylor Colridge

Samuel Taylor Coleridge

Samuel Taylor Coleridge (21 October 1772 – 25 July 1834) was an English poet, literary critic, philosopher, and theologian who, with his friend William Wordsworth, was a founder of the Romantic Movement in England and a member of the Lake Poets. Samuel was.born in the town of Ottery St Mary in Devon, England, and his father was the Reverend John Coleridge (17181781), the well-respected vicar of St Mary's Church, Ottery St Mary and was headmaster of the King's School, a free grammar school established by King Henry VIII. Samuel was the youngest of ten by the Reverend Mr. Coleridge's second wife, Anne Bowden (1726-1809). Samuel suggests that he "took no pleasure in boyish sports" but instead read "incessantly" and played by himself. A reader seemingly by instinct, Coleridge grew up surrounded by books at shoot, at home, and in his aunt's shop. The dreamy child's imagination was nourished by his father's tales of the planets and stars and enlarged by constant reading. Through this, " my mind had been habituated to the Vast - & I never regarded my senses in any way as the criteria of my belief. I regulated all my creeds by my conceptions not by my sight - even at that age." Experience he always regarded as a matter of whole and integrated response, not of particular sensations. As an adult, Coleridge suffered from opium addiction. In the eyes of many readers, his poem "Kubla Khan" was a opium-induced Orientalizing fantasia of the unconscious. His opium addiction (he was using as much as two quarts of laudanum a week) begin to take over his life: separated from his wife Sara in 1808 and quarreled with Wordsworth in 1810. It is unclear If his growing use of opium (and the brandy in which it was dissolved) was a symptom or a cause of his growing depression. In April 1816, Coleridge, with his addiction worsening, spirit depressed, and his family alienated, took residence into the house of Dr. James Gillman, a physician in Highgate, now a north London village. Gillman was partially successful in controlling the poet's addiction and Coleridge remained at Highgate for the remainder of his life.

Grey Lady

With piercing eyes, her vision stared
As if to see some unknown land
And with shuffling gait, she made her way
Without the aid of earthly hand.

Adorned with hair that templed gray
Yet long and black - pleasing still,
Belied her troubling age some say,
Still strong in spirit, iron of will.

Pale and gaunt, she walked the hall
Purposefully through the tunnel of pain
Ears hearing some unspoken call
She'll go again from whence she came.

Bones protruding beneath her robe
Gave reverence to the thing she be
And called to mind a kinship there
Yes, she belongs to you and me.

Once burdened by the agonies of life
As much imprisoned, as now she's free.
A glory gold to all behold
A shadow of eternity

R.G. Hurst

Afterword
epilogue

What makes a great poem?
What would be its attributes? In my humble opinion there are three factors.

1) It should be mysterious, since the spirit itself is mysterious in nature.

2) It should convey a message deep in nature that is not always received on first reading. At the very least it should provoke thought in the reader so he will seek out the message.

3) It should be life changing, at least in a singular discrete way and this transformation should affect the reader's mind and heart long after the poem is read.

It is my sincere hope that every single reader of these poems is transported into a new and deeper reality. God bless you all.

R.G.Hurst

www.ingramcontent.com/pod-product-compliance
Lightning Source LLC
LaVergne TN
LVHW081528060526
838200LV00045B/2040